Just Horses

Just Horses

PHOTOGRAPHY BY DENVER BRYAN
TEXT BY MARGOT PAGE

WILLOW CREEK PRESS

MINOCQUA, WISCONSIN

Published by Willow Creek Press
P.O. Box 147
Minocqua, Wisconsin 54548

Photographic prints of images appearing in *Just Horses* are available
through the photographer's website at www.denverbryan.com or by
writing to P.O. Box 368, Bozeman, MT 59771.

Designed by Heather M. McElwain

For information on other Willow Creek titles,
call 1-800-850-9453

Library of Congress Cataloging-in-Publication Data
Page, Margot.
    Just horses / text by Margot Page : photography by Denver Bryan.
        p.   cm.
    ISBN 1-57223-137-8
    1. Horses--Pictorial works. 2. Horses. I. Title.
SF303.P34   1998
636.1'0022'2--dc21   98-30022
                                                          CIP

Printed in Canada

Contents

AUTHOR'S INTRODUCTION

To Brooke, with love

I'd like to express gratitude to Debbie Martin, Amy Blasdale, Gwenn Perkins, Judy and Jordan Werner, Meredith Bogonovich, Liz Sevin, Sarah Maione, Richard and Sabina LaTour (Eastbrook Farm), Dave Perkins, Amy Desautels, Bob Wendell, Larry Hume, Battenkill Equine Veterinary Clinic, Trumbull Mountain Tack Shop, Northshire Bookstore, Sherri Alper, Sue Parsons, Martha Weisman, and everyone else who has helped me with Athena and with this book project.
—Margot Page

I t would not be an exaggeration to say there are a million young girls and boys across the world day-dreaming this very instant about galloping a horse across a landscape, the thrill of the animal's speed and strength beneath them creating a rising bubble of joy in their hearts.

Or else they're dreaming about sharing a quiet moment with a hungry pony and a carrot.

Or imagining an arcing stream of water sluicing away dark sweat from the magnificent sculpture of the horse's body as defined in glistening, wet detail.

These are the images that horse-crazy people like myself carry with us, even into adulthood: the unknown adventure that beckons when a leafy trail unfolds between the eagerly pricked ears of your mount, your fellow pilgrim. Or the peace that envelops you when perched on an upside-down bucket in a stall, listening to the lazy munch of hay, a moment of respite in a busy adult world.

All of us know who we are. We are horse nuts — whether we get a lump in our throats watching a supreme equine athlete run his great, glorious heart out on a racetrack, feel a soaring sense of liberation when a pastured horse capers and gyrates in a coltish, awesome display of pure animal release — or whether we just experience a private, holy moment of communion with a large beast.

We all share a mythical, spiritual connection with this magnificent, breathtaking creature known as the horse . . . ancient symbol of myth and realism, elegance and rawness, sublime beauty and transcendent power, control and freedom.

Just listen to the storied legends of history and literature:

Pegasus. Bucephalus. The Trojan horse.

Black Beauty, Ginger, and Merrylegs. Flicka. Black Gold. Misty of Chincoteague. Stormy. The Black and Napolean. National Velvet.

Man o' War. War Admiral. Whirlaway. Citation. And perhaps the greatest race horse of all time, Secretariat.

Their very names bring chills of awe or a rush of warm memory. They take flight in our collective imaginations, these fabled horses of myth and lore.

I, too, was one of the legions of dreamy, horse-crazy kids – collecting the ubiquitous horse statues, studying the various breeds (and finally settling on the Palomino as the most beautiful and romantic of all), jamming the rigid plastic legs of my Barbie astride my plastic herd, and looping ordinary belts around my four-poster bed so that I could imagine I was driving a team of horses and a wagon train through a terrible storm. My obsession with horses became well-known to my sixth-grade teacher, who always kindly selected me to read aloud any passage that mentioned the "H" word. When my mother bribed me into getting another dreaded pixie hair cut with an offer of weekly riding lessons, her shameless negotiation was met with utter joy.

Then came magic years of hanging around the back-country Greenwich, Connecticut, stable where Foxtrot, Mr. Chips, Hopscotch, Butterscotch, and Coppertone stoically tolerated the daily bouncing of kids on their backs and I learned to ride. The heady smells of the barn, the sweet hay, candylike grain, even the distinctive odors of manure and horse sweat signaled my entrance into a safe, delicious, golden world, a world that was closer to the dreamworld where my true self lived than anything else in my life at the time. I withheld my barn clothes from the laundry for a few extra days so as to prolong my contact with my private Eden and was an avid reader – at age twelve – of the weekly racing column in *The New Yorker*.

I never, however, owned my own horse until a decade later. After looking for hoofprints that failed to appear in my driveway for too many Christmas mornings, when finally an official adult, I gave myself the grandest present of all for my 21st birthday, a golden horse purchased for a princely sum of $800, which, by the way, I did not possess. Luckily, the seller took pity on an impoverished horse worshipper and the payment-plan route became a viable option.

Throughout the lean years of graduate school, I scrounged a way to hay, grain, and stable my buckskin horse, Carson, somehow always managing to locate funky farmhouses with old barns to rent. Carson was a stubborn, Roman-nosed Quarter-horse cross whose mouth was as hard as asphalt and who used to rocket me around the woods of New Hampshire. After a rather protracted and wild battle of wills, we eventually made our peace and there followed many wonderful adventures and journeys together. When he died in Maryland in 1982 — mercifully, with one last clump of sweet grass in his mouth — one of the first victims of a then-new and unnamed virulent disease now known as Potomac Horse Fever, it was one of the saddest nights of my life.

It wasn't until nearly 15 years later that a horse again came into my life, under unexpected circumstances. At a soccer game, I heard about a sweet and very large Thoroughbred mare being slowly starved to death who was destined to go the knackers if a home couldn't be found for her. I fell in love with her personality and her spidery hugeness, and a week later bought her for the price of her flesh.

Two hundred and fifty pounds later, Athena is a gorgeous, healthy animal (her portrait is on page 21 [bottom]), who lives in a palace of a stable, who is doted on by her two humans — me and my 11-year-old daughter Brooke — and who brings home well-deserved blue ribbons.

When a horse gets wind under its tail, whether it be on the first crisp fall day or at the sight of a Really Scary Thing (be it a train, a cow, or a truly hideous piece of paper blowing across the paddock), nothing equals the momentary glory of its ballet: neck arched almost cobra-like, nostrils flared, eyes large and dark, tail up and streaming like the wind personified, delicate mane ribboning the air, and legs springing, their high action extended. The animal is suspended in air, its defined muscles rippling under its sleek coat.

No one witnessing these moments can do anything but stand, riveted, in silent awe of the sheer beauty of this dance.

In the pages of this book you will see images of horses and the people who care about them from across the United States. Whatever your favorite breed, Appy, Quarter, Thoroughbred, Morgan, Arabian, or any cross therein . . . this volume is about the spirit of the horse, and its unique relationship to us.

The horses in these splendid images by renowned wildlife photographer Denver Bryan almost leap off the page toward you. You can smell the sweat and the barn odors, sense the electricity of a nervous or curious animal. You can feel that satiny gloss of the horse's coat, the surprising delicacy of his legs, the warmth of steam coming off his body after a winter workout.

If you're a child, you can identify with the encompassing love that shines in the eyes of the children in the photographs. For many horse-crazy kids, this is their first great and glorious love. If you're an adult, perhaps you can remember those feelings – when all was possibility, when a blue ribbon was just around the corner, when the gentle worlds of *My Friend Flicka* and *The Black Stallion* were accessible at the turn of a page, and when you could believe horses and people lived forever.

Icons of splendor, freedom, and romance, horses are the stuff of dreams.

May they ever gallop through yours.

– Margot Page
East Arlington, Vermont

PHOTOGRAPHER'S INTRODUCTION

For my father, Gene Bryan,
the man who introduced me to the wonders and ways of horses.

When I was twelve years old my father finally scraped together enough money to buy an eighty-acre gentleman's farm in the countryside outside of my hometown of Columbia, Missouri. Although his real job remained in town, he moved his wife and three boys to the country and for the next half-dozen years or so I finished growing up while falling off horses . . . frequently.

I learned a lot from horses during these years. Like how a strong hand often gets you results but it doesn't get you much trust. How it's usually better to take control of a bad situation before it takes control of you. And how fear from the back of a runaway horse may temporarily paralyze you but it won't likely kill you . . . though I often wasn't convinced of this when perched atop an out-of-control horse running at breakneck speed toward barbed wire fences.

I've also discovered that horses mean different things to different people. Most people often find a friend and companion in their horse that brings them a sense of independence, and an ally in their quest for self-reliance and accomplishment. Oh, the cowboy life. Country folks find more utilitarian value in their beautiful beasts of burden while city folks find simple pleasures. Either way and for other reasons, a lot of people love horses and this book is for them.

Some of the people who I am indebted to for their generous contribution of time and patience during the photographing of this book are: Annie Beck, Nikki Morgan, Pete and Tanya Rothing, Margot Page, Brooke Page Rosenbauer, Danielle Thompson, Gwenn and Hannah Perkins, Sharlene Anderson, Liz and Danielle Smith, Megan Lyons and many other horse owners who endured my cameras.

—Denver Bryan
Bozeman, Montana

Portraits

Studies in Equus

onsider the head . . .

The etched, fine-tipped ears. The flaring, delicate nostrils. The alert, wary eyes that can flash with rage or melt you with liquid tenderness.

. . . Immortalized since a Paleolithic artist in Lascaux drew its image on the sooty walls of a cave milleniums ago. He (or she) was trying — as we still do today — to capture the power of the horse, that undefinable something that draws the human eye and heart to this living epitome of grace and strength.

Curiosity and fear . . . the warring impulses of the horse. The eyes speak volumes and so does the body language.

No closer!

Then there are benign moments, when the horse relaxes, softens. Mellows out. Yet remains watchful. Always watchful.

This is when you can approach, speak the language of Equus. Engage in the communication between man and beast, when the line between wildness and domestication blurs.

When you have seemingly irreconcilable polar opposites now blending in a delicate pairing . . . human and horse.

Among horsepeople, true appreciation of the horse lies in the rippling shoulders, the powerful haunch muscles, and the seemingly frail, but oh-so-powerful legs that drive this equine machine – in a churning of flying hooves and dirt – up to 37 miles per hour.

Consider, then, the beauty and poetry of a horse in motion, drawing its power from the ground into the very air through which it moves. Like Pegasus reborn.

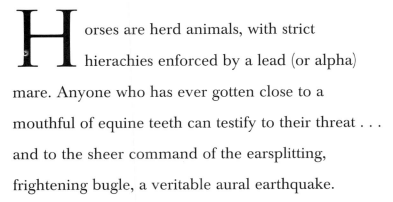

Horses are herd animals, with strict hierachies enforced by a lead (or alpha) mare. Anyone who has ever gotten close to a mouthful of equine teeth can testify to their threat . . . and to the sheer command of the earsplitting, frightening bugle, a veritable aural earthquake.

These tools – as well as lethal hooves and legendary speed – are the weapons of a prey animal that needs the well-oiled dynamics of a herd in order to survive the perils of life in the wild.

V ulnerable, spider-legged foals – like splay-
footed, ungainly toddlers – are the prodigy
comedians in the horse world. The oversized ears,
baby faces. The ridiculously long legs and
foreshortened bodies. The liquid eyes.

The coltish feints and gambols. The waggish
curiosity. Then the safety of mama, who grazes
calmly, trying to ignore the foolishness and innocent
abandon of her foal's spring of life.

Birth, nursing, bonding, these new lives are universal symbols of spring, eliciting a surprising softness in even the most hardened horseperson. In time these foals will grow into worlds of their own; they will be separated from their mothers and enter the world of man, some to enjoy lives of pampered luxury, some to not fare as well. A few lucky ones will grow old in good health, and be retired to pastures reminiscent of their youth.

B ut for now they are young and fearless, like all children of the world. There is only the present. With no thoughts of past or future, they live for that short time under the sun, in a meadow, as timeless images of fertility, maternity, and peace.

Living with Horses

Down on the Farm

Horsepeople are folks of all kinds and means. And with approximately 7 million horses in the U.S. alone today (nearly all of them are pleasure horses), equine accomodations run the gamut. From the majestic country estates with miles of four-rail fencing in classic horse country settings – where the animals seem to live better than many human beings in some parts of the world. . .

. . . to smaller, still elegant stables and barns –
complete with kids and dogs – that have managed so
far to fend off suburban development . . .

. . . to the western ranch with even more scenic acreage than its Kentucky bluegrass counterpart. (Kids and dogs also included.) Maybe you don't own those mountains but they certainly come with the territory.

What ties these geographically and economically disparate estates, stables, and ranches together are the horses that live there and the people who love and care for them. You might as well stick signs in front of every one of them that announce "Horse Lover." (Or "Horse Sucker," as some parents might mutter.)

And then there is the gear . . . the "things" that keep a barn clean and orderly and tack shops in business . . .

L iving with horses is a high-maintenance game. The work never ends, particularly when those horse apples fall like generous manna from . . . well, you get it.

Mucking stalls is the common denominator of the horse world . . . when a horse has to go, it has to go . . . whether it's in the middle of a hunter pleasure class, in front of your proper mother, or on the boots of a prospective buyer. And let's not even get into equine flatulence in the jumpers.

And horses must be fed 365 days of the year – usually twice a day – in rain, sleet or snow. No matter if you're cold, grumpy, or tired. Forget sleeping late. Or going away for the weekend. The horses are dependent on you . . . there they are, waiting for you at the gate like clockwork, ready with welcoming nickers, restless hooves, some crowding and pushing, and then – bliss! – muzzles sunk deep into grain or hay. After a time of pronounced chewing noises, then, only then, does a certain peace fall upon the hungry . . . until twelve hours later when there you go again.

Serpentines, figure eights. Leg yielding. Sitting trots, posting trots. Circles, circles. Half halts. Bending. Leg, leg, leg! Outside rein. Contact!

A horse requires regular conditioning to keep it sound, fit, and motivated. Whether the program involves long-lining, aqua therapy, a good walk, or work under saddle, the equine athlete must be cultivated with care. Mostly it's a kind of numb tedium, occasionally broken by a flash of perfection . . . that is, if you're still paying attention!

Horsedom is, if anything, humbling. It's not just the animal's sheer power, inner wildness, or the unexpected tumbles when we're feeling our cockiest.

Take, for example, the reality check that Mud Season brings. Suddenly your gorgeous horse can no longer be idealized as Pegasus. Your steed is instead, – you discover when you arrive at the barn, – covered from ear to hoof with wet, pungent mud, mixed with the pasture's manure, that has accumulated over two days of joyous rolling in the muck. Redolent smells of spring waft from the beastie's body. No more white socks, no more distinguishing blazes.

There, in front of you, is elemental animal coated with elemental earth in all its imperfect, springtime glory. And it's on your boots. And in your truck. And in the house.

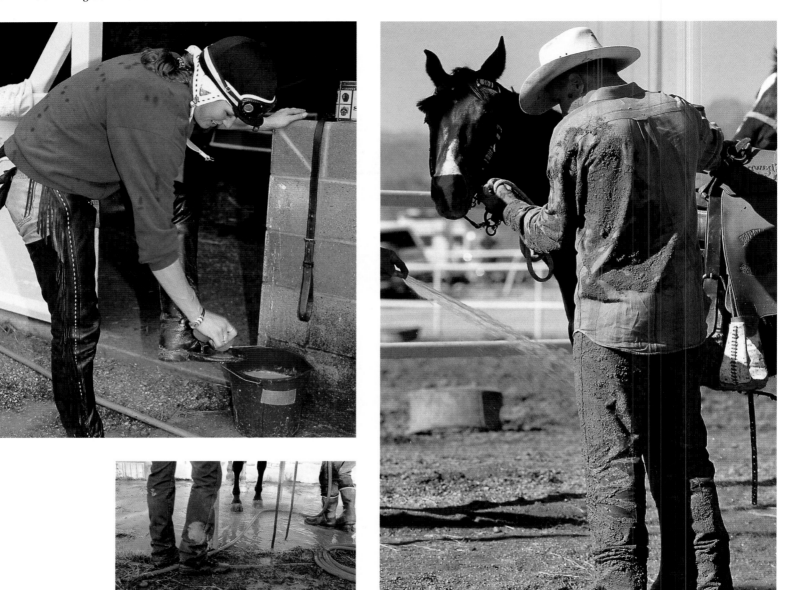

No hoof, no horse, as the old adage goes.

One of the horse's best friends is the farrier. Clip, clunk, hissss. The routine sounds of the monthly visit frame a reassuring ritual involving a patient (usually) horse – albeit a steed that is standing rather inelegantly with one leg racheted aloft – an aproned, strong-armed farrier, and a steel anvil. An old art, that of shoeing a horse where the worth of the animal was measured in direct correlation to the condition of its feet . . . uh . . . hooves.

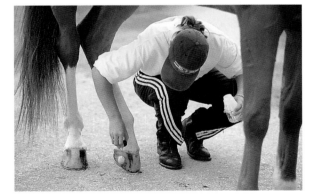

For most horsepeople and their horses, bath day is the best of all. Here is the chance to minister to your friend, to shampoo away all of the dust, dander, and grime, to make that white face really jump, to lather up a limp mane and tail into glorious fluff. Not only does the horse end up looking like a pampered courtesan, but during the soaping and rinsing, you get to delight in every glistening inch of your equine sculpture . . . and enjoy a little playtime with your buddy.

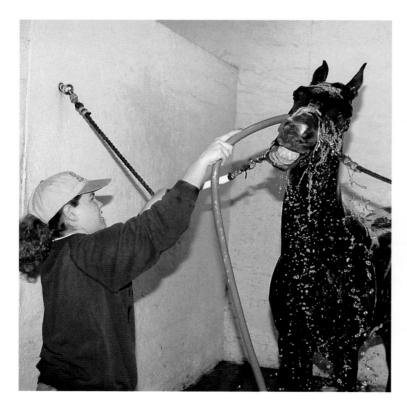

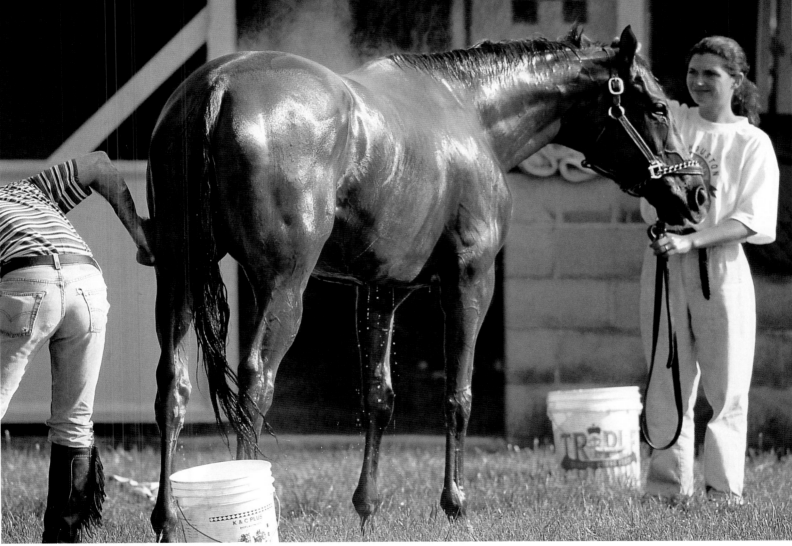

omehow, the boundaries are relaxed. Your horse seems a little less Horse and you feel a little less confined by, well, Human limitations and Human concerns.

It's a peaceful time and everyone seems to enjoy the soothing water and the sponging fun.

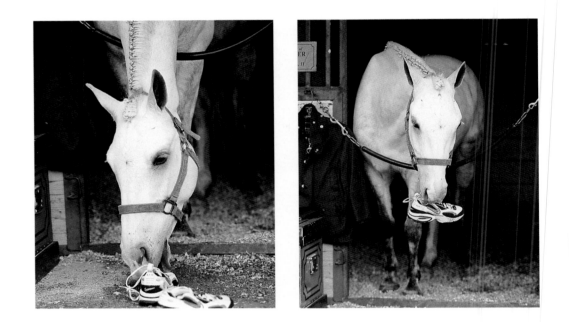

Naturally curious when comfortable in their surroundings, horses like to explore . . . their rubbery lips looking for something – anything! – interesting, especially if there's a remote possibility it might resemble a long, sweet, orange carrot. You never know . . . Anything is fair game if left within reach.

So many pockets (and buckets, feed bags, lunch . . . and dogs).

So little time.

I n contrast to their wary, explosive side, horses have the astonishing capacity to establish friendly relationships with their animal neighbors, no matter how much smaller – or furrier – they might be. Once a herd animal, always a herd animal . . . whether the new herd member be a barn dog or a barn cat.

Treat time. Apples? Yumm. Or a good head scratch? Oooh, baby. . . .

In such quiet, affectionate moments lie the rewards horsepeople seek . . . the magical trust between man and beast.

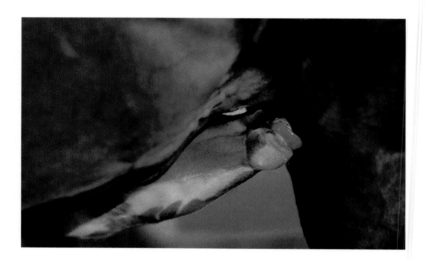

And sometimes, when life seems a bit too complicated – as when, for instance, those damned mile-long legs won't do what you want – it's important to remember the simpler things . . .

Nourishment being one of them.

The peace and strength of mother love being another.

Yuck! Whaddidya put on the bit! Next time, rinse the soap off!

And listen, while you're at it, can't you get all those straps on right the first time? So hurry up, it's time to go, enough puttering.

Let's go riding!

From the days of playing horsey – to that first good-hearted steed who carted you around, legs and elbows flapping – to the age of wisdom and experience, the lure of the horse delights young and old. It's a lifetime thing for horsepeople. Once you've gotten the horse itch, you're in it for good.

A solitary ride in the landscape is an important discovery. When it's just you and your horse on the trail, something special happens. You experience yourself in the world a different way. You become a pioneer. You gain a new appreciation for the beauty around you. You and your horse are tuned in only to each other and the surrounding environment. It's a private journey to cherish.

D uet. Take a walk to the river on a lazy, Indian summer day. Hooves paw and splash, then relax into the coolness of the water that flows around the legs . . . Silken tails float languidly downstream . . . Mirror images are reflected in the river below.

Riding with friends spreads the joy. Whether it's shared high spirits of a gallop across a field or a few quiet moments of communion, it's just plain fun . . .

. . . and there are lots of friends
out there waiting to be found.

Working Horses

Horse Power
and Beasts of Burden

I n the animal kingdom, there is no creature with a better work ethic than the horse, and the horse at work was the very muscle of our youthful nation. The word "workhorse" means stolid, dependable, with a heart and legs that won't quit. In America, the workhorses known as Quarter Horses (descended from Spanish stock introduced to America in 1600) literally built the West — transporting the explorers and pioneers who expanded the frontier, establishing cattle ranches, herding cattle to market . . .

. . . and thus was created the quintessential American icon, the cowboy and his horse.
Weathered, lean, laconic. Tough and independent. All of which could describe the
horses as well as their riders. (Except for the tobacco-chewing habit.)

From long, dusty days of wrangling, chasing, roping, and branding those little
doggies in the land of John Wayne and Gary Cooper . . .

. . . to harsh winter days where only the rugged need apply – riding fences, dropping hay, or moving herds to lower pastures. To see the Quarter horse at work is to witness living American history . . . complete with its traditions of a romantic past.

But you will also still find the working horse in other arenas, always exemplars of endurance and spirited power: on the farm, in the woods, in parks and on urban streets, ploughing fields, bringing in the maple sap, hauling logs, patrolling to make streets safe.

They serve as dependable pack horses or on a string of riding horses at dude ranches . . . there to carry greenhorns across terrains of juniper and sagebrush too imposing for man on foot. Or through mountain meadows best appreciated (some say, *only* to be appreciated) from the back of a horse.

The Competitive Horse

*In the Ring, At the Rodeo
and Around the Track*

The Show. It's just that. A show of your talent. An exhibition of your horse's training, ability, beauty. A chance for you both to shine in front of the world.

It starts with practice. You work for hours after school on balance, stamina, pacing. Those endless figure eights, 20-meter circles, barrel work. It's slews of mistakes, oceans of patience, and day-after-day conditioning to build you and your animal up to the highest level.

And it's dreams at night of a clean run, of a blue ribbon fluttering in your horse's bridle. Of applause and hoots of congratulations. Of work and sweat and fine athletics well rewarded.

T he day arrives. You've spent most of the day before the event polishing your tack to a gleaming luster, rounding up the various gear you need to bring: manure forks, buckets, coolers, fly spray.

But most of all, like an Egyptian handmaiden to her queen, you've pampered your mare, lavishing on her a spa-quality beauty treatment . . . bathing and shampooing, bleaching socks, oiling hooves, braiding manes and tails, every plait an emblem of affection and pride . . .

B eneath the various outfits required by competition – whether they be britches or chaps, Stetsons or hard hats – lies a grit and steely determination that will single out the toughest-minded and best-trained rider of them all. No matter the size of the competitor . . . the heart is harder to measure.

Competition can range from riderless halter classes in which the conformation and turn-out of the horse is judged as one would a sculpture or painting, with microscopic attention to detail of a decidedly specialized equine nature. Overall symmetry, the underline, the head, shoulders, legs, chest, the topline. Soundness . . .

. . . to informal games of sometimes breathtaking ability and wild play where the child in all of us is unloosed (if you look really closely, you can see the white knuckles of mothers along the fence).

The second-most important team other than horse and rider is parent and rider.

All moms and dads know the drill. Hold your breath, make the sandwiches, walk the horse . . . Take orders from your kid . . . Hang over the fence feeling that strange sensation of your heart choking your throat and shameless, indulgent pride . . . And be ready with a hug if one is needed.

I n competition there are necessary winners and losers, tears and ribbons.

The rewards lie in the bond you two share after a good ride and lessons learned, however hard they are . . . Another ribbon is always around the corner.

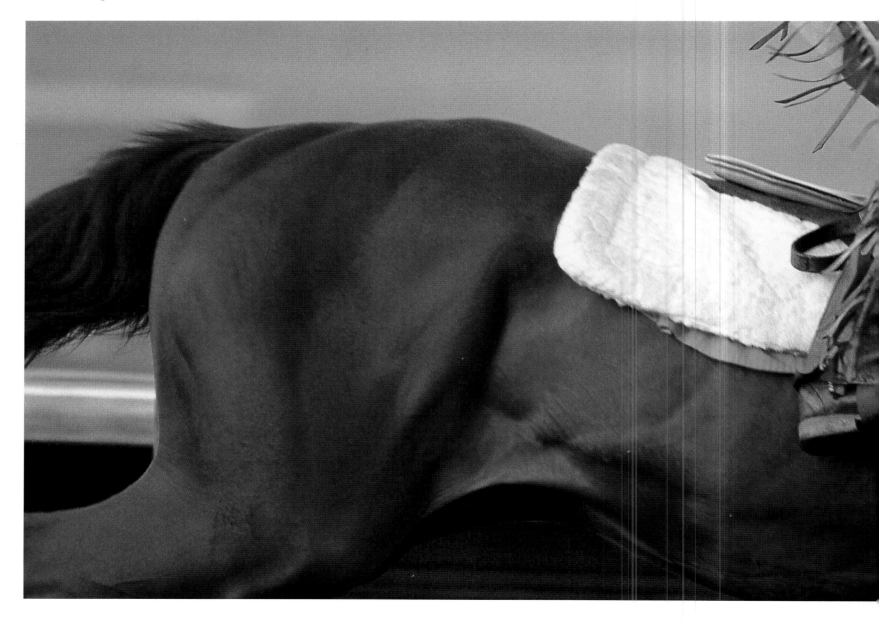

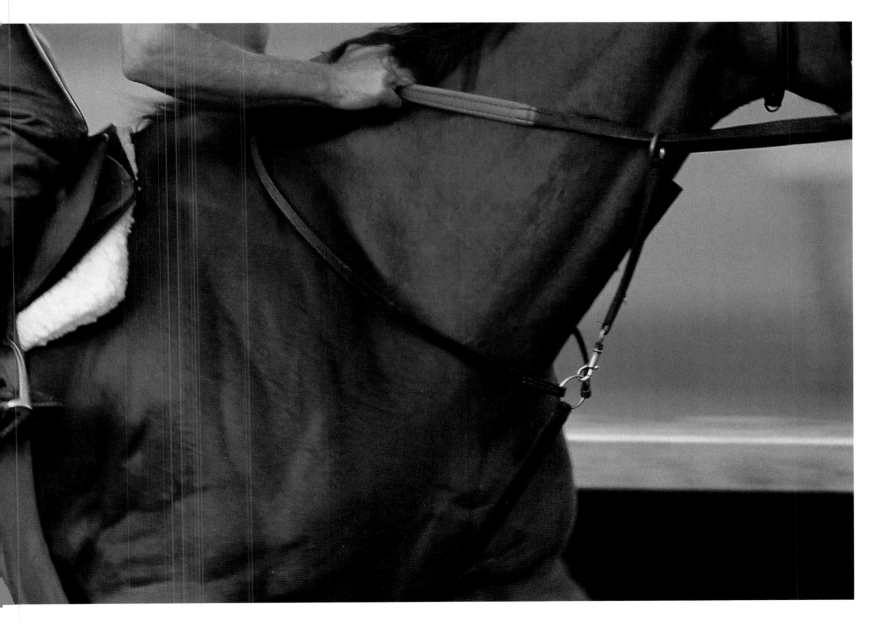

A nd then there is the sport of Kings.

Practicing the ancient art of racing are the sinewy racehorses . . . the aristocratic athletes of the horseworld. These pedigreed bluebloods team up with their jockeys in an extraordinary collaboration – a dance of blinding speed and power that embodies the essence of the horse.

But first they have to learn the rudiments of racing: how to run in company, how to run along the rail, how to rate speed, how to break from the gate. Then long gallops – called breezes – build wind, bone, tendons and ligaments.

Handling livestock is what the mighty Quarter Horse was bred for. Its sturdy strength and lightning agility make it the blue-collar worker, the all-around athlete of the horse world.

Whether it be driving cattle, roping steers, or cutting calves, the Quarter Horse – who can turn on a dime and hand you back change – has formed the backbone of the Western experience. Calm, honest, reliable – and with that distinctive, sexy butt – this breed has earned the respect of horselovers across the nation.

To mankind, the horse gave individual freedom and mobility of movement. And to our country, the horse gave us a particular brand of American heritage and culture.

Heroic stuff mixed with down-and-dirty hard work. Rodeos. Cowboys.

A singular courage when pushing the envelope.

It's what America is all about. And the horse is an essential part of that national identity.

But a national symbol inevitably invites reality . . . and the always-possible ignominy of the face-plant. For as much as we try to bend this animal's spirit to our own will, ultimately they are always – in some thankfully unreachable place inside them – unbendable . . . forever free and wild.

So back we go again for more . . . for we just can't get enough of this great-hearted, noble creature of myth and history, the horse.